D1737644

CIVILIZATIONS OF THE ANCIENT WORLD

ANCIENT GREECE

A MyReportLinks.com Book

KIM A. O'CONNELL

MyReportLinks.com Books

an imprint of

 Enslow Publishers, Inc.

Box 398, 40 Industrial Road
Berkeley Heights, NJ 07922
USA

MyReportLinks.com Books, an imprint of Enslow Publishers, Inc. MyReportLinks®
is a registered trademark of Enslow Publishers, Inc.

Library of Congress Cataloging-in-Publication Data

O'Connell, Kim A.
  Ancient Greece / Kim A. O'Connell.
    v. cm. — (Civilizations of the ancient world)
  Includes bibliographical references and index.
  Contents: The land and early history—Life of the people—
Ancient Greek government—The city-state and wars—
Great legacy of arts and culture—Alexander the Great.
  ISBN 0-7660-5250-8
  1. Greece—Civilization—To 146 B.C.—Juvenile literature. [1.
Greece—Civilization—To 146 B.C.] I. Title. II. Series.
  DF77.O25 2004
  938—dc22

                          2003027355

Printed in the United States of America

10 9 8 7 6 5 4 3 2 1

To Our Readers:
Through the purchase of this book, you and your library gain access to the Report Links that specifically back up this book.
The Publisher will provide access to the Report Links that back up this book and will keep these Report Links up to date on **www.myreportlinks.com** for three years from the book's first publication date.
We have done our best to make sure all Internet addresses in this book were active and appropriate when we went to press. However, the author and the Publisher have no control over, and assume no liability for, the material available on those Internet sites or on other Web sites they may link to.
The usage of the MyReportLinks.com Books Web site is subject to the terms and conditions stated on the Usage Policy Statement on **www.myreportlinks.com**.
A password may be required to access the Report Links that back up this book. The password is found on the bottom of page 4 of this book.
Any comments or suggestions can be sent by e-mail to comments@myreportlinks.com or to the address on the back cover.

Contents

ANCIENT
GREECE

MyReportLinks.com Books
Great Books, Great Links, Great for Research!

The Report Links listed on the following four pages can save you hours of research time by **instantly** bringing you to the best Web sites relating to your report topic.

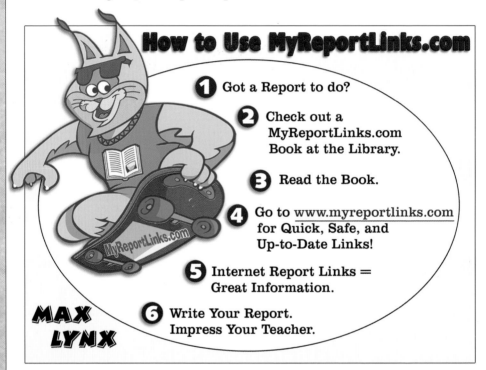

How to Use MyReportLinks.com

1. Got a Report to do?
2. Check out a MyReportLinks.com Book at the Library.
3. Read the Book.
4. Go to www.myreportlinks.com for Quick, Safe, and Up-to-Date Links!
5. Internet Report Links = Great Information.
6. Write Your Report. Impress Your Teacher.

MAX LYNX

The pre-evaluated Web sites are your links to source documents, photographs, illustrations, and maps. They also provide links to dozens—even hundreds—of Web sites about your report subject.

MyReportLinks.com Books and the MyReportLinks.com Web site save you time and make report writing easier than ever!

Please see "To Our Readers" on the copyright page for important information about this book, the MyReportLinks.com Web site, and the Report Links that back up this book. Please enter **VGR9464** if asked for a password.

Report Links

➤ **The Internet sites described below can be accessed at http://www.myreportlinks.com**

▶The Ancient Greek World
*EDITOR'S CHOICE

This Web site features information on the lands of ancient Greece. Click on "other topics" to learn more about ancient Greek culture.

▶Ancient Greek Civilizations
*EDITOR'S CHOICE

Many different groups of people, each with their own unique cultures and practices, lived throughout ancient Greece. This helpful site has information about the history of these civilizations, their cultures, the cities they lived in, and more.

▶The Ancient Olympics
*EDITOR'S CHOICE

The very first Olympic Games were held in Greece over two thousand years ago to honor the god Zeus. Here you can find out about this ancient festival, including when and where the first games were held, what the athletes were like, and more.

▶The Greeks: Crucible of Civilization
*EDITOR'S CHOICE

This Web site provides biographies of several people who helped shape ancient Greece into a thriving empire. You can also view an interactive map of the region.

▶The Cradle of Western Civilization
*EDITOR'S CHOICE

On this Web site, you can learn about ancient Greek mythology, philosophy, government, cities, and influential people.

▶The Persian Wars: Greece's Finest Hours
*EDITOR'S CHOICE

The Persian Wars marked a turning point for the Greek Empire. This Web site, made specifically for kids, explains what happened during these wars and discusses the aftermath of this power struggle.

Report Links

The Internet sites described below can be accessed at http://www.myreportlinks.com

▶**Ancient Greece**

This page contains all kinds of information about ancient Greece, including facts about geography, mythology, art and architecture, the Greek people, and the Olympic Games.

▶**Ancient Greece**

This site provides an introduction to the clothes worn in ancient Greece, with helpful pictures and explanations.

▶**Ancient Greece—History for Kids!**

Ancient Greece was one of history's largest and most well-known empires. At this Web site designed for kids, you can find out about Greek history, religion, government, people, and many more interesting topics.

▶**Ancient Greece: The Persian Wars**

In 490 B.C., the Persian Army attacked the Greek city-state of Athens, which marked the beginning of the Persian Wars. This brief summary gives information about different battles, important people, and the outcome of the Persian Wars.

▶**Ancient Greece Time Line**

The Greek Empire lasted for several thousand years. This time line breaks down the major events in Greek history from 6500 B.C. to A.D. 286, including battles, conquests, and literary achievements.

▶**Ancient Greek Cities**

Ancient Greece contained several large city-states. Here you can read about some of these, including Athens, Sparta, Corinth, Olympia, and more.

▶**Battle of Plataea**

The historic Battle of Plataea marked the end of the wars between the Persians and the Greek city-states. This site describes how the Greeks triumphed over the Persian Army and brought an end to these wars in 479 B.C.

▶**The British Museum**

This British Museum Web site offers a virtual tour of its collection of Greek and Roman antiquities. Click on "galleries" to find a list of images.

Report Links

**The Internet sites described below can be accessed at
http://www.myreportlinks.com**

▶Exploring Ancient World Cultures: Greece

This site offers a brief introduction to the culture of ancient Greece and provides links to the literary works of Plato, Aristotle, and Aristophanes. It also contains links to other sites that feature images of ancient Greek art.

▶Greek Alphabet

The alphabet used by the ancient Greeks (as well as Greeks today) is a lot like the one that we use, with similar letters and similar sounds. Learn about this alphabet and what it looks and sounds like at this Web site.

▶Greek Art and Architecture

This helpful Web site contains numerous pictures and descriptions of Greek artistic and architectural achievements. You can view ancient temples and palaces as well as sculpture from thousands of years ago.

▶Greek Pottery—The Origins of Greek Pottery

Ancient Greece produced some of the most unique works of art ever created. Much of what we know about ancient Greek art comes to us through pottery. This site describes the origins of Greek pottery and describes different kinds of pottery.

▶GreekLandscapes.com—Ancient Greece

Ancient Greece's world-famous architectural achievements are known for their elegance and style. At this site, you can see pictures of these landmarks, such as the Parthenon and the ruins at Delphi.

▶Hercules: Greece's Greatest Hero

Ancient Greece is famous for its legendary epic stories and heroes. One of the most famous heroes is Hercules. Here you can learn about Hercules, what he is said to have done, and why he is such an important part of Greek culture.

▶Met Time Line: Balkan Peninsula

This interactive time line from the Metropolitan Museum of Art offers images of ancient Greek art as well as links to more information about the culture of ancient Greece.

▶Mythweb

Life in ancient Greece was affected by its mythology of gods, goddesses, and heroes. Learn about these rich cultural beliefs and stories at this site.

Report Links

The Internet sites described below can be accessed at http://www.myreportlinks.com

▶**National Archaeological Museum of Athens**

For centuries, Greece has produced some of the most renowned pieces and styles of art and architecture. This Web site, sponsored by the National Archaeological Museum of Athens, includes various art collections from different periods in Greek history.

▶**Odyssey Online: Greece**

This Web site from Emory University offers a look at the people, mythology, daily life, burials, and writings of ancient Greece.

▶**Peloponnesian War**

In 431 B.C., growing tensions between Athens and Sparta erupted in what is known as the Peloponnesian War. At this Web site, you can read a summary of the events of this war and its eventual outcome and find links to related topics.

▶**Philip of Macedon**

From 359 to 336 B.C., the region of Macedonia in ancient Greece was ruled by King Philip II, father of Alexander the Great. At this Web site, you can learn about Philip II's life as ruler, his conquests, his family, and his death.

▶**Philosopher of the Week—Aristotle**

Aristotle, who lived in ancient Greece from 384 to 322 B.C., is one of the most well-known philosophers in the world. Learn about his life, ideas, and contributions to the world of philosophy at this comprehensive Web site.

▶**Socrates**

Socrates was a Greek philosopher who greatly contributed to the understanding of science and the world around us. This brief biography offers an account of the life of Socrates.

▶**The Trojan War**

The legend of the Trojan War is based on an actual battle between the ancient Greeks and the city of Troy. This historic legend is summarized at this Web site, which includes information on its origin, the actual battle, and the people involved.

▶**A Voyage Back in Time: Greece and Rome**

This site about ancient Greece and Rome offers a glimpse into what life was like in these ancient civilizations. You can learn about agriculture, government, music, entertainment, family life, and much more.

Any comments? Contact us: **comments@myreportlinks.com**

Time Line

1250–1184 B.C.	The war that will provide the basis for the legendary Trojan War is probably fought.
800 B.C.	Greeks develop an alphabet and build early temples.
700–500 B.C.	Archaic Age in ancient Greece.
776 B.C.	First Olympic Games are held.
750–700 B.C.	City-state political system emerges; the *Iliad* and the *Odyssey* are written; period of lyric poetry begins.
550 B.C.	Sparta becomes dominant on the Peloponnese.
507 B.C.	Cleisthenes reforms Athenian constitution; democracy develops.
500–449 B.C.	Persian Wars: Battles of Marathon, Thermopylae, Salamis, and Platea; Athens emerges as most powerful city-state in Greece.
490 B.C.	Beginning of the Classical Age and style in art and sculpture.
461–431 B.C.	Golden Age of Athens under leadership of Pericles.
447–432 B.C.	The Parthenon is constructed in Athens.
431–404 B.C.	Peloponnesian Wars between Athens and Sparta are fought.
404–377 B.C.	Sparta rules as the most powerful city-state in Greece.
347 B.C.	Plato founds the Academy.
342 B.C.	Aristotle begins teaching Alexander, son of King Philip of Macedon.
338 B.C.	Philip of Macedon defeats Athens at battle of Chaeronea; conquers Greece.
336 B.C.	Alexander succeeds Philip upon his death.
334–333 B.C.	Alexander defeats Persians at battles of Granicus and Issus; cuts the Gordian Knot.
332 B.C.	Alexander conquers Egypt.
327–325 B.C.	Alexander invades Northern India.
323 B.C.	Alexander dies; his generals vie for power.
323–143 B.C.	The Hellenistic Age marks shift toward multiethnic population and culture.

THE LAND AND EARLY HISTORY

The landscape of ancient Greece made it highly unlikely that a great civilization would develop there. There were too many mountains, no major rivers where water and rich soil allowed people to grow enough food, and no vast open plains where a civilization could flourish.

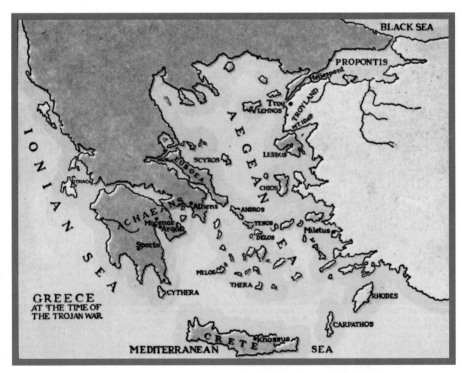

▲ Ancient Greece at the time of the legendary Trojan War, c.1200 B.C. This period is known as the late Mycenaean, and it marked the beginning of advances in Greek culture.

Covering the southern part of the Balkan Peninsula, ancient Greece was rugged and hilly. About three quarters of its territory was mountainous, and only about a quarter of the land along the coast and small valleys was suitable for farming.

Ancient Greece had three distinct geographical regions. Northern Greece included portions of ancient Macedonia and low-lying coastal plains. Central Greece was capped by the highest point in Greece, Mount Olympus, believed to be the home of the gods, and Athens, the capital of modern-day Greece. Southern Greece included the Peloponnese, a peninsula that thrust into the Mediterranean Sea. It housed another great ancient city—Sparta. Southern Greece was connected to central Greece by a narrow isthmus at Corinth. Ancient Greece also boasted numerous islands sprinkled throughout the Aegean Sea, an arm of the Mediterranean Sea between Greece and Turkey. Two of the largest islands, Crete and Rhodes, were mostly mountainous.

The climate of ancient Greece was semiarid, with long, hot summers and short, rainy winters. The weather varied greatly from region to region, ranging from long periods of drought to heavy, flood-causing rainstorms. The lack of adequate rainfall along the hilly landscape meant the ancient Greeks could not produce enough food to support themselves.

The Aegean and Mediterranean seas also dramatically impacted the lives of the ancient Greeks. Most of the region was near the seas. It was easier for the Greeks to travel by sea than over the rugged, mountainous landscape. They also traveled the seas to settle on the islands off the mainland where they established colonies along trade routes to secure the goods they needed.

The lion gate, part of the citadel walls of Mycenae, was built during the third stage of the fortress's construction in 1200 B.C. The gate protected the palace and administration buildings as well as homes.

▶ Early Settlers

The territory of ancient Greece was populated as early as the Stone Age, when humans survived by hunting and gathering food, using tools made of stone, wood, and bone.

One of the first major civilizations that developed in this region was the Minoan. It developed about 3000 B.C., on the island of Crete in the Mediterranean Sea. The Minoans ruled that part of the world until about 1450 B.C. However, the Minoans were not Greek.

The first ancient Greek civilization began around 2000 B.C. during the Bronze Age, when wandering tribes migrated south into the Balkan Peninsula. This civilization is known as the Mycenaean, named after the city of Mycenae in the Peloponnese. The Mycenaeans were warriors and sailors who took control of the region, including the island of Crete, where the non-Greek Minoans had created a wealthy civilization. The late Mycenaean period, from 1400 B.C. to 1100 B.C., was marked by cultural advances and the beginnings of classic Greek mythology.

The Mycenaean kingdoms were regional states, each ruled by powerful kings and warlords from fortified palaces, called citadels. The mighty walls of the citadels were ten feet thick and surrounded by the fields and villages of farmers and craftsmen—all controlled by the king. At its height, the Mycenaean civilization was powerful and wealthy. This civilization was considered to be an age of warrior heroes, but it lasted only about three hundred years.

At one time, people dismissed the stories of early Greek history as myths. However, in the late nineteenth century, a series of archaeological digs revealed great Mycenaean palaces surrounded by massive walls, archives written on thousands of clay tablets (in a script called Linear B by scholars), elaborate wall hangings, and elaborate tombs with skeletons covered with gold and jewels. Other excavations uncovered evidence that the Trojan War—one of Greece's most beloved myths—was actually based on a real war.

The Trojan War

Archaeologists believe that the Trojan War was based on a conflict fought around 1200 B.C. between invading Greeks of Mycenae and the people of Troy, a prosperous city on the east coast of the Aegean Sea in what is today Turkey. Although the exact history may never be known,

most Greek understanding of the Trojan War comes from Homer, one of the greatest Greek poets. He described the Trojan War in two epic poems, *The Iliad* and *The Odyssey*.

According to mythology, the Trojan War began when Paris, the Trojan prince, kidnapped Helen, wife of Menelaus, the king of Sparta. When the Trojans refused to return Helen, Menelaus persuaded his brother King Agamemnon of Mycenae to lead an army against Troy. The Greeks sent a fleet of a thousand ships to Troy to recapture Helen. The war waged on for nearly a decade, until the Greeks destroyed Troy after deceiving its citizens by hiding soldiers in the Trojan horse.

Dark Age and Renaissance

By 1200 B.C., the cities of the Mycenaean civilization were destroyed and the palaces of the great kings were burned. Historians are not sure why this civilization declined so rapidly. The Dorians from northern Greece invaded around 1100 B.C. and occupied these cities that had been weakened by war. Thucydides, an Athenian historian from ancient times, described the end of the Mycenaean civilization in this way: "The return of the Greeks from Troy after such a long time caused many changes; in general, there was civil strife in the cities, and exiles from these founded other cities. . . . And eighty years after the War, the Dorians occupied the Peloponnesus with the Sons of Heracles."[1] Heracles, or Hercules, was a mythical Greek hero known for his feats of strength.

This threw ancient Greece into a period of decline known as the Dark Age that lasted about four hundred years, until 800 B.C. The advanced communities of the Mycenaeans disintegrated after the Dorian assault, and Greeks lived in small, isolated villages, growing just enough food for their own families. The art of writing disappeared, and most record keeping ceased. After producing a rich variety of cultural artifacts in previous periods, the Greece of the Dark Age left behind little evidence of its culture. Most historians believe this was a period of migration that dispersed Greek citizens to settle new colonies. The Greeks established colonies west of the Greek mainland in what is today Italy. They also formed colonies in the eastern Aegean. These colonies were called Ionia. These Greek colonists were separated from the political and religious communities of the mainland.

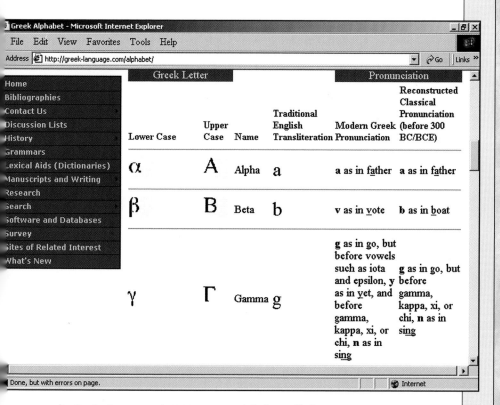

Greek Letter			Pronunciation		
Lower Case	Upper Case	Name	Traditional English Transliteration	Modern Greek Pronunciation	Reconstructed Classical Pronunciation (before 300 BC/BCE)
α	A	Alpha	a	a as in father	a as in father
β	B	Beta	b	v as in vote	b as in boat
γ	Γ	Gamma	g	g as in go, but before vowels such as iota and epsilon, y as in yet, and before gamma, kappa, xi, or chi, n as in sing	g as in go, but before gamma, kappa, xi, or chi, n as in sing

Beginning around 1300 B.C., an alphabet called Linear B was used in ancient Greek texts. However, writing disappeared in Greece after 1200 B.C. until the late ninth or early eighth century B.C. when texts written in Linear A (shown here) appeared.

By 900 B.C., Greek civilization began to recover. Pottery was produced more often and featured more complex designs. After a period in which subjects were limited to animals and geometric figures, Greek art began to feature human activity again, possible evidence of a renaissance, or rebirth, in Greek culture and society. The most significant cultural contribution of the Greek renaissance occurred around 800 B.C. when the Phoenician alphabet was adopted to write the Greek language. The Greek alphabet consisted of twenty-four letters and is still used in Greece. The term "alphabet" comes from the first two Greek letters, *alpha* and *beta.* The alphabet spread to all parts of the Greek world and helped unite its people culturally.

▶ The Rise of the Greek City-State

Toward the end of the Dark Age of Greece, the population increased and small villages became cities. Greek communities called city-states began to develop. A city-state, called a *polis,* consisted of a city or town and its surrounding farmland and villages. Each city-state was independent of the others and each had its own history, economy, culture, and type of government. The citizens of each polis often quarreled among themselves and seldom acted together except when they were threatened by invasion.

By around 700 B.C., there were more than a thousand city-states in the Aegean area. Ancient Greece was not a single, unified country. Even though the ancient Greeks spoke a common language, they had no single leader, unlike the civilizations in ancient Egypt and Persia. Two of the most advanced city-states were Athens, on the Attic plain, and Sparta, in the Peloponnese.

LIFE OF THE PEOPLE

Although Greece is known as the birthplace of democracy, for much of its history ancient Greece had a very divided society—with a distinct upper class and a lower class. The upper class was made up of aristocrats, wealthy land owners who controlled most of the city-states. The lower class

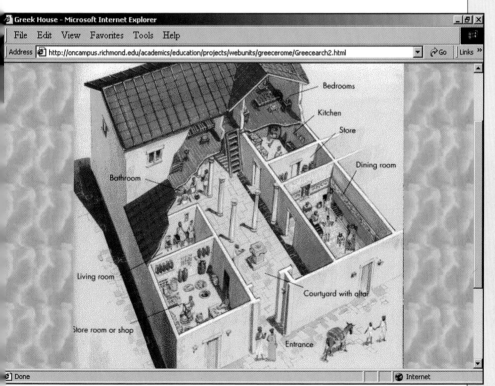

Greek House - Microsoft Internet Explorer

File   Edit   View   Favorites   Tools   Help

Address http://oncampus.richmond.edu/academics/education/projects/webunits/greecerome/Greecearch2.html   Go   Links

Bedrooms

Kitchen

Store

Dining room

Bathroom

Living room

Courtyard with altar

Store room or shop

Entrance

Done   Internet

▲ Ancient Greece's upper classes could afford luxurious homes with many rooms centered around a courtyard. A mosaic would often adorn the floors and walls of these homes with sand and colored pebbles from the beach.

was made up of peasants and slaves. Peasants were commoners who lived under the rule of the aristocrats. Peasants were technically free, but they were often indebted to their landlords. Slaves were sometimes owned by the government and placed in supportive roles such as police officers or secretaries. Private slaves would either work on farms or tend to household chores.

The aristocrats were known as *hoi agathoi,* or "the good," while the peasants were called *hoi kakoi,* or "the bad." Another term for this class was *hoi polloi,* which is still used today to describe the common people of a society.

Although ancient Greece was a class-oriented society, wealthy and poor citizens lived in similar style homes. Family homes were simple wood, mud brick, or stone buildings, with a series of rooms arranged around a courtyard. These structures included an *andron,* which was a men's dining room that was decorated or had a marble floor. Buildings were often painted a bright white to reflect the hot Mediterranean sun.

The arrangement of private houses offers an example of early urban planning. In most Greek city-states, the city center included a dense concentration of private homes, which were connected by narrow streets and broken up by garden plots. All the private and public buildings were arranged around an open space, called an *agora,* where community meetings were held and goods were offered for sale.

▷ Farming and Clothing

Although only a small portion of Greece could be farmed, the Greeks did successfully cultivate the "Mediterranean triad" of crops—grain, grapes, and olives. From these, Greeks made bread, wine, and olive oil, which were the staples of their diet and are still popular in modern Greek cuisine. The ancient Greeks also ate peas, beans, fruits, and nuts in abundance. High-protein foods such as cheese, meat, and fish were also eaten, but in smaller quantities, almost as a relish for the meal. The Greeks did not like butter and drank little milk, preferring water or wine instead. Honey and spices were used to sweeten or season foods.

Greek farmers also kept flocks of sheep, goats, and pigs. Oxen and mules were valued for plowing and pulling loads, and cattle were raised for their meat and hides. Only the

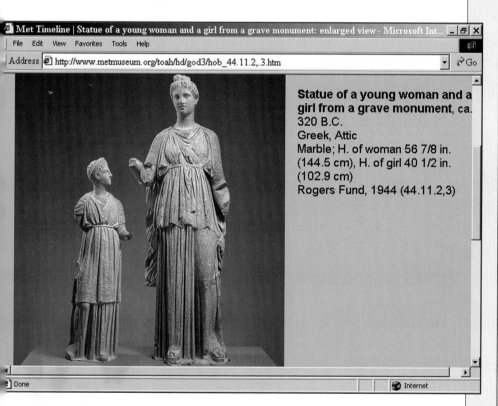

Met Timeline | Statue of a young woman and a girl from a grave monument: enlarged view - Microsoft Int... _ ☐ X

File   Edit   View   Favorites   Tools   Help

Address http://www.metmuseum.org/toah/hd/god3/hob_44.11.2,.3.htm   ▾ ⟲ Go

Statue of a young woman and a girl from a grave monument, ca. 320 B.C.
Greek, Attic
Marble; H. of woman 56 7/8 in. (144.5 cm), H. of girl 40 1/2 in. (102.9 cm)
Rogers Fund, 1944 (44.11.2,3)

Done   Internet

▲ The Doric peplos was the garment worn by women in ancient Greece before the sixth century B.C. The figure on the right wears the peplos over an Iconic chiton, a garment worn by the women of ancient Greece after the sixth century B.C.

Large Image - Microsoft Internet Explorer

File   Edit   View   Favorites   Tools   Help

Address =1&_IXMAXHITS_=1&_IXSPFX_=graphical/full/lg&_IXimg=ps209715.jpg&submit-button=summary   Go

Done   Internet

▲ *These figures play a game of knucklebone. Similar to the modern-day game of jacks, knucklebone involved throwing pieces made of sheep or goat anklebones in the air and catching as many as possible with one hand. This game was especially popular among children.*

members of the upper class kept horses, which were used for riding and pulling chariots.

The clothing of the ancient Greeks was simple but well suited to the climate and the surroundings. Made by the women of the household, as well as any female slaves, most clothes were rectangular in shape and required little sewing. Men wore simple tunics of linen or wool, while women wore long garments called *peplos,* which were gathered at the waist and pinned at the shoulders.

Trade

Because the seas were close to almost all parts of ancient Greece, trade became an important part of life for the Greeks. Greeks built cargo ships to export any surplus products, such as olive oil and wine. They traded among the Greek islands and with colonies that were overseas as well as with foreign lands.

Family Life

Modern understanding of Greek family life comes primarily from Athens, which preserved family rituals in vase painting, tomb sculptures, and dramatic stories. In Greek society, before citizens could become members of the polis, they first had to be accepted into a family group, known as the *oikos*. Fathers determined the fitness of the child upon birth and decided whether the child would be kept or abandoned. If the child was healthy and accepted, the happy news was announced with the hanging of olive wreaths or tufts of wool on the front door. If children were abandoned, they would sometimes be raised and sold as slaves. Once accepted into a family group, a boy would also be approved for membership in his father's *phratry,* or brotherhood, which was a clan of relatives that protected each other.

Men usually married when they were thirty years old, while women usually were married at age fifteen. Women came to the marriage with a dowry, a gift of money or property, for her new husband. During the wedding, the bride's father would say to the groom, "I give you my daughter to sow for the purpose of producing legitimate children," to which the groom would agree by saying, "I take her."[1] Greeks often married members of their own family. Household duties were divided: outside work for

the men, including plowing and planting, and inside work for the women, including sewing and cooking.

Education

Greece's two rival city-states, Athens and Sparta, had very different ideas about how youth should be educated. In ancient Athens, education was for the wealthy aristocrats. The purpose of education was to train children in the arts and literature. Girls were not allowed to attend school, but they were taught at home to read and write. After some home schooling, boys were often sent to a small neighborhood school where they memorized famous passages written by Homer or taught to play a musical instrument called the lyre. Other subjects might include reading, writing, math, and playing the flute. In their teens, boys went to a high school and then to a military school, graduating around age twenty. The upper class could afford to send their children to private tutors.

In Sparta, education centered almost entirely on military training. At the age of six or seven, Spartan boys were sent to military school, where they lived in barracks and trained to be warriors. To toughen them up, boys were forced to go barefoot and sleep on rough mats, and stealing was encouraged. At the end of their teen years, males had to pass a test of their fitness and military skills to become a soldier. If they failed, they were banished to the middle class. Similarly, Spartan girls were sent to military schools where they were taught wrestling, gymnastics, and combat skills. If their women were strong, Spartans believed, they would produce strong babies— the soldiers of the future.

Gods and Religion

Ancient Greeks believed that many gods and goddesses directed their everyday lives. In Greek society, citizens worshiped their gods at traditional altars, often making ritual sacrifices of animals. The earliest Greek religions were actually a mix of elements from Asia and Egypt. Eventually, through various works of literature, the wide range of Greek gods and goddesses began to be clearly organized. Myths were written about their origins and activities. In Homer's *Iliad,* the gods were portrayed as a tight-knit family group, residing on Mount Olympus. The remarkable aspect of the ancient Greek religion was

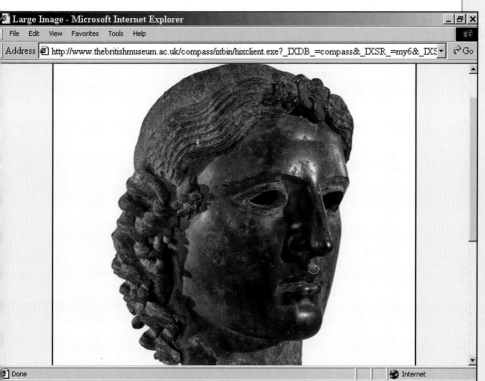

Large Image - Microsoft Internet Explorer

File   Edit   View   Favorites   Tools   Help

Address http://www.thebritishmuseum.ac.uk/compass/ixbin/hixclient.exe?_IXDB_=compass&_IXSR_=my6&_IXS   Go

Done   Internet

▲ *This unusually large bronze head, dating from 460 B.C., is believed to represent Apollo, the god of prophecy, music, medicine, and poetry. Sculptors of the time usually represented only gods as bigger than life size.*

that the gods were given human traits and displayed human emotions and weaknesses. These gods and goddesses resembled humans, but they were immortal and had special powers. Each god represented a different human trait or force of nature. Citizens appealed to these gods for help in their lives, and city-states often adopted a god or goddess as its representative.

Throughout the ancient world, there were shrines, called *oracles,* where ancient Greeks could seek advice from the gods. They believed that Delphi was the center of the world and many of them made pilgrimages to seek advice from the god Apollo, often identified with the sun, who lived there. People consulted a priestess who would go into a trance and pass messages to and from the gods. These messages were often difficult to interpret.

Zeus, god of the heavens and defender of justice in the universe, was thought to be the leader of the Olympians. According to myth, Zeus had many wives and companions, but the most famous was Hera, the most beautiful Olympian. Zeus also had many powerful children. Among them were Aphrodite, the goddess of love; Ares, the god of war; and Persephone, goddess of the seasons. In one of the most famous myths, Zeus' son Heracles was forced to perform twelve tasks, or labors, including wrestling a lion and killing a multiheaded snake called the Hydra.

ANCIENT GREEK GOVERNMENT

The ancient Greeks introduced the idea of a democratic form of government, one in which ordinary citizens participated directly in decision making. The word *democracy,* or rule of the people, comes from two Greek words: *demos,* which means "people," and *kratos,* which means "strength" or "rule." Democracy was just one form of government practiced by the ancient Greeks.

▲ Aristotle (right) tutored Alexander the Great between 342 and 340 B.C. Scholars disagree whether the philosopher, a student of Plato, believed democracy to be the best form of government. Their opinions are based on Aristotle's thirty philosophical treatises that survive.

The Polis

The centerpiece of ancient Greek government until 338 B.C. was the polis or city-state. City-states were independent and self-governing. In ancient Greece, this meant that city governments could range from absolute monarchies—led by a single ruler—to democracies ruled by the vote of the people.

Greek city-state governments usually consisted of an assembly and a council. In democracies, assemblies were the primary political power, composed of citizens. In oligarchies where a few powerful people ruled, the council had the final say, representing the small group of leaders—usually a family unit—that held power. Although city-states sometimes combined into larger religious or military organizations, most were constantly in danger of attack by other city-states. For example, Greece's two most powerful cities—Athens and Sparta—had very different styles of government. Their intense rivalry led to the devastating Peloponnesian War.

At first, small city-states required few officers. Athens had several dozen officeholders at the end of the sixth century. A century later, that number had increased to about seven hundred political officers. Political offices were not organized into hierarchies, although the chief officer was usually called the *archon,* which means "leader," or *prytanis,* which means "president."

Athenian Democracy

Athens was the true birthplace of democracy, which began around 507 B.C. when an Athenian statesman named Cleisthenes came to power. Democracy developed gradually and slowly over the next two hundred years. Cleisthenes, an aristocrat, proposed a constitution in which all male adult citizens automatically became

The teachings of the ancient ▷ Greek philosopher Plato have had a profound influence on Western civilization.

members of the assembly. At that time, there were about thirty thousand members. On important matters the entire assembly met to decide the issues. The assembly elected a council of five hundred men who directed the government's daily business.

For the first time, ordinary citizens, who were not aristocrats or rich, could participate. But the Greeks had a limited definition of *citizen*. Only men, eighteen years of age or older, of Greek origin were considered citizens and therefore allowed to vote; women, children, and slaves were not. In addition, a person's social status factored heavily in his participation. In Athenian politics, the wealthier and more socially connected the candidate, the more likely he could gain office. Citizens over the age of thirty could serve as jurors on the people's court.

Another reform allowed the assembly to banish citizens from political activity. This process was called *ostracism*. Each man took an *ostrakon*, or pottery shard, and wrote on it the name of a citizen whom he wished to exile. If one person received more than six thousand votes

against him, he was banished from Athens and not allowed to return for ten years. Some of the city's greatest heroes were ostracized because the Athenians grew jealous of their power and influence.

The fundamentals of democracy instituted by the ancient Greeks have endured and are still practiced in the United States and other democratic societies in the world. They include the decision of a majority vote, the right to a trial by jury, and the ability to question or even recall political leaders. Celebrating democracy, Euripides wrote that, in Athens, "Our city is not subject to one man. No, it is free, for here the people rule."[1]

▶ The Spartan Mix

Sparta's government was a mix of monarchy, democracy, and oligarchy. Spartans favored keeping political power in the hands of a monarch or a council of elders. However, Sparta eventually saw the value in creating a system of checks and balances so that the government could not easily take a swift, radical action. To achieve this, Sparta created a dual-king government. Not only did the two kings cooperate on political issues, but they also protected Sparta from ever being without a ruler. The council included the two kings and a group of twenty-eight elders who prepared material for the assembly. Sparta also established an assembly of citizens—all men over the age of thirty—who could accept or reject proposals, but were not allowed to discuss them. Unlike Athens, there were no people's courts in Sparta.

THE CITY-STATE AND WARS

Although its name implies something old or outdated, the Archaic Age of ancient Greece (700 B.C.–500 B.C.) produced some of Greek society's most influential cultural contributions. It was during this time that the Greek city-state form of government took hold. This was also a time of colonization. The lack of adequate farmland forced the Greeks of the

The Ancient Greek World - Microsoft Internet Explorer

File   Edit   View   Favorites   Tools   Help

Address http://www.museum.upenn.edu/Greek_World/   Go

© 1996 Univ. of Pennsylvania Museum

Attic Red Figure Bell Krater
ca. 430-410 BC
By the Dinos Painter

(57 items remaining)   Internet

▲ *This red-figure vase depicts four young men resting after a hunt.*

Archaic Age to explore the Mediterranean from one end to the other, establishing hundreds of colonies along the way.

Art, architecture, literature, and philosophy all flourished. Two dominant artistic techniques—called "black figure" and "red figure"—emerged, in which silhouettes were painted on pottery in one color or another, with details cut into them. These innovations greatly increased international trade and extended the Greek influence.

However, with the strengthening of Greek city-states came increasing conflicts among them. On the Peloponnese, the three city-states of Sparta, Argos, and Corinth began to fight over territory. Despite this, the Archaic Age spurred a greater sense of cultural unity among Greek city-states, which would be strengthened in the coming wars against Persia.

The Persian Wars

Between 500 B.C. and 449 B.C., Greek city-states fought four major battles against the powerful Persian Empire, which included all of western Asia and Egypt. Under the tyrannical rule of King Darius I, Persia had hoped to invade and add the Greek city-states to its vast domain. Many of the city-states united together to ward off the invaders.

In 490 B.C., a Persian expedition planned an attack on Athens. Both armies met on the coastal plain of Marathon, twenty-six miles northeast of Athens. Even though they were outnumbered two to one, the Athenians defeated the Persians in a decisive battle, slaughtering more than six thousand Persians. According to legend, a messenger ran nonstop the twenty-six miles from Marathon back to Athens to announce the victory. After delivering his message, he collapsed and died from exhaustion. Today, in honor of that legendary run, the distance of the race known as a marathon is 26.2 miles long.

Ten years after Marathon, the Persians launched another massive invasion. It was led by Darius' son, King Xerxes I. The king ordered two bridges made of ships to be built and tied side by side so that his armies could cross over the Hellespont, a strait that separated Asia from Europe. The Persian Army, with more than three hundred thousand soldiers, outnumbered the Greek Army of only ten thousand soldiers. Led by King Leonidas of Sparta, the Greek Army went north to defend the narrow mountain pass at Thermopylae, a strategic location that served as the gateway to southern Greece. Here is where the Persians would cross to invade Athens and Sparta. A traitor told Xerxes about a mountain pass that would position the Persians behind the Greeks. When Leonidas realized he was trapped, he dismissed all the soldiers except three hundred men from his Spartan city-state. The Spartans, bound by a pledge to fight, did not retreat. Instead, they

This statue shows the goddess Athena holding Zeus' head. Athena, the daughter of Zeus and Metis, was a guardian of Athens, where the Parthenon was erected as her temple.

A naval commander and statesman, Themistocles arranged for the evacuation of Athens before Xerxes' invasion, saving countless lives.

attacked the Persians. Every single Spartan soldier, including Leonidas, was killed. This is known as one of the most heroic battles in world history. The Persians continued on and conquered Athens, much of which they burned down.

By this time, Athens had developed the greatest naval force in ancient Greece under the direction of Themistocles. He ordered a fleet of two hundred *triremes,* warships that were quick and easy to maneuver. Shortly after Thermopylae, Themistocles lured the Persian fleet into a narrow channel off the island of Salamis. The triremes fought and devastated the Persian Navy. This was the turning point in the wars with Persia. In the final battle that took place at Plataea, the well-trained Spartan forces defeated the remaining Persian land forces.

After these victories, Greece became united when Athens formed the Delian League, in which about two hundred city-states agreed to cooperate with each other in common defense against the Persians. As a result of the wars, Athens became the most powerful city-state and Sparta became the second most powerful. The victory over the Persians was a turning point in the history of ancient Greece. It saved Greece from foreign rule. Historians still debate how different the world would be if Xerxes had conquered Greece and it had become part of the Persian Empire.

An Ancient Rivalry

The two very different societies of Athens and Sparta sparked one of the key rivalries of ancient Greece.

Athens was named for Athena, the Greek goddess of wisdom and war. Athena was a fitting symbol because ancient Athens witnessed both outstanding cultural, political, and intellectual achievements and long periods of warfare and strife. Athenian leaders encouraged development of the arts and literature and fostered an open, democratic society.

Sparta was a rigid society whose ruling class enforced discipline, simplicity, and obedience. Spartan citizens trained for war from an early age and remained soldiers all their lives. Today, the word *spartan* is still used to describe something that is disciplined, restrained, or basic.

Athens had the strongest naval power; Sparta had the strongest and most disciplined land power. Athens headed the Delian League. Suspicious of Athens' growing power, Sparta formed the Peloponnesian League. These two rivals struggled to dominate the ancient Greek world.

The Peloponnesian War

A war between Athens and Sparta began in 431 B.C. Early in the war, it appeared that the Athenian fleet had the upper hand, winning several victories. However, about 430 B.C., a plague killed nearly one quarter of the population of Athens, including its leader, Pericles. Sparta conquered several Athenian cities in successful military campaigns, including a decisive victory at Amphipolis in 422 B.C. Eager to punish

▲ *Greece at the time of the Peloponnesian War.*

its old enemy, Persia helped Sparta to assemble a fleet to fight the Athenian Navy. This first fleet was destroyed, but another Spartan fleet won a key naval battle. Despite their losses, the Athenians repeatedly declined offers to make peace. Finally, under the command of Lysander, the Spartan fleet destroyed the Athenian Navy in 405 B.C., forcing Athens to admit defeat and surrender the following year. The war changed Sparta from a distrustful, isolated city-state into a world power.

Some historians believe that Sparta's greed and self-serving power contributed to both its own decline and the weakening of traditional Greek society as a whole. As the Greek orator Isocrates wrote, "[I]n some citizens, power was the cause of injustice, depravity, disrespect for the laws and greed for riches."[1]

Chapter 5 ▶

GREAT LEGACY OF ARTS AND CULTURE

Throughout the modern world, one can see the influence of ancient Greece, whether through replicas of ancient Greek temples, the continuing tradition of the Olympic Games, or in poetry and the arts. Ancient Greece can even be heard in our language: Many English words and phrases are derived from Greek roots.

Many, but not all, great achievements came during the Classic Age (500 B.C.–400 B.C.) and particularly during the Golden Age of Greece under Pericles, the leader of Athens.

▲ The Parthenon was built in Athens between 447 and 432 B.C. to replace two other temples on the Acropolis honoring Athena. This structure represents the city-state's growing domination of Greece as well as the power and influence of its builder, the statesman Pericles.

The Golden Age was brief, lasting only thirty years. It began after the Persian Wars, when Athens had to rebuild, and ended when Sparta defeated Athens in the Peloponnesian War. During this era, Athens rose to economic and political supremacy to becomes the most powerful city in the ancient world. It was the center of a trade network for goods from all over the world. The Athenians produced great art, architecture, literature, and philosophies.

Pericles was a statesman who had a great vision for Athens. He wanted Athens to become a city that would lead an empire. Pericles believed that the ideal citizen should participate in his city's government. He felt that politics was the business of every citizen. During his rule, Pericles spent large sums of money on massive reconstruction projects, especially public buildings that everyone could use: gymnasia, theaters, law courts, and public dockyards.

Art and Architecture

Greek cities were often planned around a tall hill called an acropolis, which was reserved for grand temples to the gods. Greek temple architecture has influenced builders and designers through modern times. Greek temples featured a rectangular structure with a porch on one or both ends that was flanked with vertical columns. One famous example of this style is the Parthenon, a marble temple in Athens that Pericles had built and dedicated to Athena.

There were three styles of columns, distinguished by the top part of the columns called the capitals. These capitals were called Doric, Ionic, and Corinthian. The capital of the Doric column is plain; the Ionic has scrolls; and the Corinthian has carved stone leaves. Examples of these styles can be seen in many public buildings today. In Washington, D.C., alone, Doric columns can be found on the Lincoln Memorial, Ionic columns on the Jefferson Memorial, and Corinthian columns on the U.S. Supreme Court building.

Pediments, or gables, of temples were decorated with sculptures of gods and goddesses, carved to look like perfectly formed human beings. Those on the Parthenon show the birth of Athena and a contest between Athena and Poseidon, the Greek god of the seas.

Literature and Philosophy

Ancient Greece also produced two of the most studied works of literature in world history—Homer's *Iliad* and *Odyssey*—that serve as a model for most epic poetry produced ever since. Epic poems are long stories about national heroes that were written in verse and usually sung or recited before an audience. Sappho was a Greek poet who wrote about friendship, love, and nature.

This bronze statue of Poseidon, Greek god of the seas and one of the most important figures in Greek mythology, dates from about 460 B.C.

The Greeks also created the idea of plays. They wrote and performed comedies, tragedies, and satires. The three best-known dramatists were Aeschylus, Sophocles, and Euripides. Early Greek dramas involved dialogue between a lead singer and a Greek chorus. In the plays of Aeschylus, the chorus played a central role by commenting in poetic language on the action. Later works increased attention on the dialogue and conflict between individuals, which is still the primary interaction in theatrical productions. Greece's foremost comedic writer was Aristophanes, whose plays were performed at festivals to honor Dionysus, the god of wine.

Ancient Greeks also established the careful practice of writing history, led by historians Herodotus and Thucydides, who recorded wars and other important events in Greece's history.

Greek philosophers had a love of learning and questioned and discussed everything in the universe. They believed that reason and philosophy rather than emotion and rhetoric should rule people's lives. In philosophy and politics, the works of Plato and Aristotle have been among the most influential in Western civilization. Plato advocated an ideal society that sought beauty and truth. Plato was a student of the great philosopher Socrates, who taught young men in the Athenian marketplace by asking questions and engaging them in dialogues to try to solve difficult problems. Socrates taught that wisdom is knowing that you know nothing. Plato's works try to recapture the style and ideas of his former teacher. He is known for his great work *The Republic,* in which he states that the ideal form of government is one led by philosophers. Plato's own student, Aristotle, later founded a school called the Lyceum, which fostered a scientific appreciation of the natural world.

Science, Mathematics, and Medicine

The ancient Greeks replaced gods with reason to explain forces in nature. Archimedes was a scientist who found that the volume of an object can be measured by the amount of water it displaces. It is said that he discovered this while taking a bath. Euclid, a mathematician, explained his ideas about geometry in a book titled *Elements,* which is the basis for modern geometry textbooks. Hippocrates, known as the "father of medicine," believed diseases had natural causes that could be treated. Today, doctors pledge the Hippocratic Oath to practice medicine according to his ideals.

The Ancient Greek World - Microsoft Internet Explorer

File   Edit   View   Favorites   Tools   Help

Address http://www.museum.upenn.edu/Greek_World/   Go

View of the Sanctuary of Pythian
Apollo at Delphi

Done   Internet

Delphi was considered to be the center of the world in ancient times. It was home to the Pythian Games, the forerunner of the Olympic Games, as well as the famed Oracle and the Sanctuary of Pythian Apollo (shown here).

▲ *This arched entryway leads to the original Olympic stadium.*

▷ The Olympics

The first Olympic Games were held in ancient Greece as early as 776 B.C.—the basis for the modern Olympics that are still celebrated today. In ancient times, the Olympic games were a religious festival held every fourth summer at Olympia, in honor of Zeus. More than forty thousand people came from all parts of the ancient Greek world, traveling hundreds of miles to attend. This was the largest gathering of Greeks in time of peace. Ancient Greeks were serious about sports, and training for the games was intense. Competitors were required to practice for ten months before they were allowed to participate in the games.

The earliest Olympic competitions were not team events. The sports events were for the individual and included running, the pentathlon (an event that combined five sports), wrestling, boxing, chariot racing, and foot racing with armor. Because they could neither compete nor even watch the Olympics, Greek women staged their own version of the Olympics called the Heraea to honor Hera, the wife of Zeus. The winners of the Olympics and the Heraea were awarded crowned wreaths of olive leaves and earned fame throughout Greece. To win was the highlight of a person's life. The Olympics celebrated the Greek ideals of the well-rounded individual: a sound, or healthy, body, and a sound mind. The Olympics continued until A.D. 393 and were revived in Athens in 1896, thus carrying an ancient Greek tradition into modern times. In 2004, the summer games returned to Athens for the first time in more than a century, featuring events in twenty-eight different sports.

The Greek lyric poet Pindar wrote several odes in praise of the ancient Olympics. "But if, my heart, you wish to sing of contests," he wrote in 476 B.C., "look no further for any star warmer than the sun, shining by day through the lonely sky, and let us not proclaim any contest greater than Olympia."[1]

Chapter 6 ▶

ALEXANDER THE GREAT

Perhaps no individual soldier in world history was as feared and respected as Alexander the Great, one of the heroes of ancient Greece. By the age of thirty, Alexander the Great had expanded the Greek empire and conquered most of Asia. In one bold campaign after another, Alexander put down uprisings around Greece and occupied surrounding cities. He was especially eager to seek revenge on Persia, which had invaded Greece 150 years earlier.

Alexander was born in 356 B.C., the son of King Philip II of Macedon and his wife, Olympias. Macedon was an ancient kingdom of northern Greece. Philip was himself a fierce soldier, conquering enemy states and expanding and training the Macedonian Army. His goal was to conquer Greece and all of the Persian Empire.

While still a teenager, Alexander commanded the Macedonian cavalry that helped his father to win a key victory at Chaeronea in 338 B.C., thus conquering Greece. Under Philip's rule, the city-state system of ancient Greece collapsed as the Macedonians established a centralized monarchy that stretched across Greece.

As the son of a king, Alexander also learned important lessons off the battlefield. He grew up under the guidance of the country's greatest teachers, including Aristotle, the famous writer and philosopher. After his father was assassinated in 336 B.C., Alexander ascended to the throne, becoming king of Macedon.

Alexander the Great was one ▶
of the world's most successful
military and political leaders.

Alexander quickly set his sights on Persia. Alexander's troops engaged in a battle at Granicus, in what is now Syria. Alexander was nearly killed in that battle. After a fierce and deadly cavalry clash, Alexander claimed victory, executing thousands of Persians. He later sent three hundred Persian suits of armor back to the Greek city of Athens with a message reading, "From Alexander, the son of Philip, and the Greeks, except the Spartans."[1] That message showed Alexander's anger at the people of Sparta, who had refused to join his campaign against Persia.

From Granicus, Alexander moved on to the city of Gordium. There he was shown the famed "Gordian Knot," a complex knot tied by a Greek king. An ancient myth stated that whoever could untie the knot would rule all of Asia. According to legend, Alexander the Great did not untie the knot, but impatiently sliced through it swiftly with his sword. Ever since, the saying "to cut the Gordian knot" means to solve a difficult problem with a single, quick, decisive action.

After conquering Persia, Alexander led his army on a march that would be one of the most memorable in world history, reaching as far as India. But Alexander made

many enemies along the way. Some Greeks criticized Alexander for his policies on intermarriage and tolerance toward other races and cultures, such as Asians.

In 323 B.C., Alexander was planning a sea voyage when he became ill and died, at only thirty-three years old. After his death, Alexander's generals argued about how to divide his empire. They divided it into three sections: Macedonia (which included Greece), Babylonia, and Egypt. Eventually, continual warfare weakened Greece.

Alexander the Great is still considered one of the greatest rulers of the ancient world, extending the vast Greek empire to the farthest boundaries of Persia, north to Russia, east to India, and south to Egypt. At the time of his death, he ruled the largest empire the world had ever seen. He remains a lasting symbol of ancient Greece—whose widespread influence in the arts, architecture, and politics can still be seen today.

Alexander and the Hellenistic Period

When Alexander the Great came to power, he successfully expanded Greek civilization and culture across much of Asia and India. Yet, in doing so, Alexander also introduced new cultures to Greek society, changing it forever. Under his reign, Greek city-states became members of a "cosmopolis"— a world of city-states that were no longer self-contained political units.

Alexander's death in 323 B.C. ushered in the Hellenistic Age of ancient Greece in which people from other nations embraced Greek intellectual ideas and artistic contributions. Although this period could be seen as a flowering of Greek culture, it was also marked by increasing internal disorganization and fighting among those who were Alexander's successors.

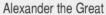

 This relief, located in the Parthenon, depicts ancient Greek horsemen riding through Athens to the Acropolis in the Panathenaic Procession, a festival celebrating the birthday of the goddess Athena. It reminds the modern world of ancient Greece's grandeur and rich culture.

Seizing the advantage, the Romans were able to conquer much of the ancient Greek Empire. By 146 B.C. the Romans were in control of Greece. Although the rise of the Roman Empire ended Greece's long reign as a political and cultural power, the influence of ancient Greece would continue to be felt around the world for many centuries to come.

Chapter 1. The Land and Early History

1. Thucydides, *The History of the Peloponnesian War,* Book 1, Chapter 12, "The Internet Classic Archive," n.d., <http://classics.mit.edu/Thucydides/pelopwar.html> (April 27, 2004).

Chapter 2. Life of the People

1. Sarah B. Pomeroy, et. al. *Ancient Greece: A Political, Social, and Cultural History* (New York: Oxford University Press, 1999), p. 235.

Chapter 3. Ancient Greek Government

1. Sarah B. Pomeroy, et. al. *Ancient Greece: A Political, Social, and Cultural History* (New York: Oxford University Press, 1999), p. 355.

Chapter 4. The City-State and Wars

1. Jacob Burckhardt, *The Greeks and Greek Civilization* (New York: St. Martin's Press, 1998), p. 293.

Chapter 5. Great Legacy of Arts and Culture

1. Pindar, translation by Diane Svarlien, *Odes* (1990), available from the Perseus Project, n.d., <www.perseus.tufts.edu> (December 7, 2003).

Chapter 6. Alexander the Great

1. Sarah B. Pomeroy, et. al. *Ancient Greece: A Political, Social, and Cultural History* (New York: Oxford University Press, 1999), p. 403.

Further Reading

Bardi, Matilda. *Ancient Greece*. Columbus, Ohio: McGraw-Hill Children's Publishing, 2000.

Chrisp, Peter. *Alexander the Great*. New York: Dorling Kindersley Publishing, Incorporated, 2000.

Cobbold, G.B. *Hellas: A Short History of Classical Greek Civilization and Its Predecessors*. Sandwich, Mass.: Wayside Publishing, 1999.

Coolidge, Olivia E. *The Trojan War*. Boston: Houghton Mifflin Company Trade & Reference Division, 2001.

Greenblatt, Miriam. *Alexander the Great and Ancient Greece*. Tarrytown, N.Y.: Marshall Cavendish Corporation, 1999.

Houle, Michelle M. *Gods and Goddesses in Greek Mythology*. Berkeley Heights, N.J.: Enslow Publishers, Incorporated, 2001.

Nardo, Don. *Ancient Greece*. Farmington Hills, Mich.: Gale Group, 2000.

———. *Women of Ancient Greece*. Farmington Hills, Mich.: Gale Group, 2000.

———. *The Decline and Fall of Ancient Greece*. Farmington Hills, Mich.: Gale Group, 2000.

———. *Leaders of Ancient Greece*. Farmington Hills, Mich.: Gale Group, 1999.

Spies, Karen Bornemann. *The Iliad and The Odyssey in Greek Mythology*. Berkeley Heights, N.J.: Enslow Publishers, Incorporated, 2002.

Index